IN SEARCH OF HEFFALUMPS

Uni Victoria Anholt

Illustrations by Cynthia Bassett

Beeberry
Books

UP PRESS
1944 UNIVERSITY AVE.
E. PALO ALTO, CA. 94303
TEL: 328-3944

CONTENTS

INTRODUCTION

"Piglet, I have decided something."

"What have you decided, Pooh?"

"I have decided to catch a Heffalump. . .
I shall do it," said Pooh, after waiting a
little longer. "By means of a trap. And it
must be a Cunning Trap, so you will have to
help me, Piglet."

Carefully, Pooh Bear contemplates a Heffalump hunt.
His imagination had been stretched by Christopher Robin's
casual report of having seen one running along and by
the fact that Heffalumps are quite rare. Pooh eagerly
designs a capture plan with friend Piglet's loyal
support. Together they lump through the chapter.

I, too, was intrigued by the idea of catching Heffalumps in A. A. Milne's classic, Winnie The Pooh, and began
a similar search with young children. Along the way we
had many adventures as we looked for those mysterious
entities.

The hunt began in 1972 when I organized a room
and a small group of children. My daughter was just two
when I decided to combine being with her and caring for
other little ones as well. That unique arrangement
provided us with an income and also let us enjoy those
early years together. In a short time that room grew

beyond my original hopes as we moved to a large building on ten acres and eventually became "Heffalump," a parent cooperative children's center. After six years our total involvement numbered over 300 children and parents and a dozen staff members.

Pooh and Piglet never captured a Heffalump. Like their hunt, ours had many surprises. After years of searching, we made many wonderful discoveries and found that Heffalumps indeed exist. Now I am delighted to share In Search of Heffalumps with you!

Uni Victoria Anholt
Palo Alto, California
November 1980

ACKNOWLEDGEMENTS

Thank you,

Cynthia Bassett for the illustrations and cover design,
Mary Ann Anholt for numerous typings,
Lisa McCann for proof reading and editorial suggestions,
Jess Wells and Peggy Kass at Up Press, for quality printing,
The Stanford students at Ecology House for donating
The Little Room space,
Colin Campbell, Dean Underwood, and Bill Smith
at St. Mark's Episcopal Church for giving us a
room and room to romp,
Bernie Trilling for patience, understanding, and good humor,
Oriana for inspiring the search and being with me
from the very beginning,
And all the children, parents, staff, and friends who
were the Heffalump adventure!

Additional Books may be obtained from:

>Beeberry Books
>Box 3888
>Stanford, CA 94305

Please enclose a check for $5.95 , plus
one dollar for handling.

For Oriana,

FIRST YEAR

Once upon a time a little room for little children grew and grew and grew . . .

The story began quite simply and like many tales unfolded with a special quality. That quality took the form of a search. For me, the search was a personal one and also a shared adventure involving many others.

It all started when I chose to stay with my two year old daughter, Oriana, and to care for other young children as well. Instead of beginning a career or returning to graduate school, I decided to create a place for small children where they would feel secure and at the same time be encouraged to explore. In the beginning I decided not to use my home because I felt Oriana and I needed our own living space, separate from the group.

I began hunting for a suitable place and by good fortune met Judy Landfield who had run an informal play-group for preschool age children in her dormitory at Stanford University. She had discontinued it and urged me to talk with her friends at Ecology House, which was an independently run residence organized around political and environmental issues. After numerous talks and a whole house meeting I was given half of their library area. I was happy to have the little room and was ecstatic as I left the meeting. I thought to myself that soon the Stanford students would be seeing tricycles parked among their ten-speeds.

When I began thinking about the space it was not with the purpose of forming a school and acting as a teacher. If anything my philosophy at that time was one of deschooling. I had read Ivan Illich, Paulo Freire, John Holt, listened to alternative school rhetoric since the mid sixties, and taught at Summerhill West when I first came to California. I was looking toward creating something different than the traditional nursery school. I saw the Stanford place as not being a school for students but a little room for little people that would belong to them.

I was also influenced by psychological theory in the writings of Erik H. Erikson, Bruno Bettelheim, Fritz Redl, Selma Fraiberg, Clark Moustakas, and had seen their developmental ideas applied in a residential treatment center for emotionally disturbed children in Chicago. Working there I had first hand experience in a program that was designed to provide a therapeutic and predictable environment. I wanted to apply my experiences with some of those practices in my current involvement with normally developing young children.

With the children I wished to build a physical and psychological milieu that was sensative to their needs and respected them as children with the same rights as people of any age. I did not want to institutionalize their learning but hoped to offer a place where exploration, acceptance, and love would flourish. Keeping those objectives in mind, I felt the energy needed to convert a ten foot high, gray and born room into such a place as an immense challenge.

One gray wall was quickly painted pumpkin orange and a clock with large numbers and a sweep hand was lowered to a spot three feet from the floor. A set of wooden hooks for coats was also hung at children's level.

The major work done in the room during those three weeks was the construction of a loft. That was something I made as much for myself as for the children. While building and learning new skills, I gained personally as I saw my ideas becoming concrete. A new sense of confidence emerged as I completed a project I had never dreamed possible. In two weeks the loft was standing and looked as if it had been built from a plan. Actually plans developed from the materials I could find. The protective railing around the top came from Ori's outgrown crib, and the slide was constructed from a hardwood door found at the dump. The amount spent was less than fifteen dollars.

When finished, the loft was rectangular and fit into a corner of the room with two sides exposed. One and a half sides were protected by the railing and the other half was open for a ladder and the slide which ran down to a solid bookcase on the floor. A carpenter helped me with the finer points of construction and another friend stapled odd shaped carpet scraps to the top and sides. Last, a brightly colored curtain was hung around the bottom enclosing an area filled with soft pillows. Using power tools and seeing the loft progress was exciting, but I will never forget feeling it come alive the first day the children saw it.

However, before everyone arrived I spent the last few weeks filling the room. Bernie Trilling, a student in the house, gave us a table and chairs set he had made for

children. The table consisted of a plywood top with
rounded edges attached to sturdy crates. In a
corner I set up cubby spaces for each child's lunch,
shoes, and miscellaneous treasures. They were simply
designed from boxes with dividers which once held large
bottles of wine. I hung spider plants and ferns in the
windows and tacked animal and book character posters to
the walls.

In deciding what kinds of things to include in our
little room I made a conscious decision not to use
toys that were a part of many children's bedrooms. I
avoided Creative Playthings, Mattel, and Fisher Price.
Instead I chose materials that could be explored and
manipulated in many ways. I wanted the children to make
their own play so that they would interact with each
other and learn the beginnings of sharing and cooperating.
I hoped everyone would gain those valuable experiences
through a garden, art projects, cooking, dress up, field
trips, stories, make believe, and drama.

With those ideas and limited also by a small budget, I
began looking for free or inexpensive materials. I made
several trips to San Francisco, the Palo Alto dump, and
various thrift stores. Each place magically seemed to
have just what I needed.

On the sidewalks of Chinatown, one late afternoon, I found many sturdy, wooden boxes. As I loaded
them into my car an old man stopped and asked me by
gesturing widely with his hands if I wanted a bigger
box. I nodded yes thinking of my plans for an indoor
sandbox. In a few days that large box was lined with
plastic and filled with sand, cups, funnels, and sifters.
The smaller boxes were painted bright colors and

supplied with scissors, glue, markers, magazines, paper
yarn, fabric, play dough, tape, and many other materials.
I stored the boxes in the bookcase just under the slide
so that all of those things would be available to the
children at any time.

The local dump was another good place to find useful
objects. Every time I drove in I discovered something
wonderful. One day as I backed my car to the edge I
found a hardwood rocking chair that only needed minor
repairs, a child's size wheelbarrow lacking two screws,
and a spring horse without ears!

Thrift stores also proved very valuable. There I
found great items for the dress up basket. I chose hard
hats, purses, football jerseys, frilly dresses, and
hiking boots. I made an effort to include all types of
articles so that all kinds of make believe could happen.
Later I learned that the children enjoyed small sized
costumes best. I also bought a workable typewriter, a
pair of real phones, and a mirror to go in the dress up
corner. In those days I was a purist for genuine playthings. For aesthetic as well as ecological reasons I
avoided plastic.

When the room was nearing completion I began to
think of announcing our opening. I did not want to
be a center or a group or a nursery school. I thought
about it carefully one day while up in the loft, and realized that what we were was a "little room." So I quickly
designed bright yellow posters listing the hours and
activities of Little Room. I put them in places I
frequented: Plowshare Books, Whole Earth Truck Store,
New Age Foods, Whole Earth Bakery, the Coop, Keplers,
Institute for the Study of Nonviolence, and various

locations on the Stanford campus. Through the posters
and by word of mouth children began joining. I received
one phone call from a Stanford student. When I asked how
old his child was he became quite embarrassed; he had
been interested in the Little Room group for himself.
I reread the poster and realized that I had never spec-
ified an age. I simply wrote "A little room for little
people" and the listed activities could be enjoyed by
any age person. I told my friend Fred Moore about the
incident and he laughed saying that I had just received
the highest compliment. Fred was influencial and also
helpful to me in examining practically as well as phil-
osophically what I was doing as I organized Little Room.

I spent some time preparing for the children.
There were certain areas of preschool education which
were totally unfamiliar to me. Looking back now I feel
that this was probably an advantage because I could use
my own intuition. I did, however, visit a half dozen large
centers and nursery schools in Palo Alto. I gained
much useful information but came away with a stronger con-
viction that young children need a warm, secure environment and also interaction with a small rather than large
group. I went to book stores looking for the latest on
early childhood education and began reading. I encount-
ered this subject in many places and was amazed at its
sudden entry into my life. I soon attended two events
devoted to children and education--the first one
was Penninsula School's Learning Fair and the other was
Rivendell School's Alternative School Conference at
Foothill College. At both those places I came in contact
with new ideas in education and met some people who have
since become close friends.

In October I attended Penninsula School's Learning
Fair. I was curious before going because the workshops
seemed interesting and I had once sent the school a teaching
application from Chicago after reading New Schools' Exchange.
The first person I met was Mike Young with his wonderful
sunflower smile. Wearing a yellow hard hat and yelling
loudly he demonstrated how triwall cardboard could be cut
with an electric saw. I was intrigued by him and his nonstop
spiel about the revolutionary effects of lowly triwall.
He spoke about how teachers could use it to affect personal
curriculum changes as they created nontraditional learning
environments. As he talked about the durability, low cost,
and politics of triwall he constructed tables, chairs, and
bookcases before a small audience. Then he turned off the
saw and asked me what I wanted to make. I think I surprised him
when I quickly answered, "A rocking chair." The night before
I had read Janet Lederman's book, Anger and the Rocking Chair,
which is an emotion-filled dialogue between a teacher and her
students. I felt a small rocking chair would be a special
addition to Little Room. We leafed through a pattern book
and designed something from cradle and chair plans. After
a little sketching I cut out four pieces. They fit together
into a rocking chair resembling a free-form pear with a
square seat. After the glue dried a child sat in it and rocked.
It worked! Later I redesigned the chair so that two children
could rock together, back to back.

    At the fair I attended many other workshops. Shira
Barnett and Jim Kerr talked about "Kids Teaching Kids," which
was a student-tutorial program within a public high
school. Peter Sessions lead a music theory workshop called
"The Glass Bead Game." Bob Albrecht had some computers and
games for children from the People's Computer Company. And

Ron Jones improvised a learning experience and distributed
Zephyros Primers. I went to a dance workshop, had an
Alexander Method session, and bought a magazine called The
Big Rock Candy Mountain. By the end of the first day I was
weary and saturated with information. The next morning I
simply returned to the fair and folk danced and made an
easel with Mike. Since I did not know the size of my paint
containers he offered to bring the circle cutter and visit
Little Room.

At the Rivendell conference on alternative education,
I participated in several workshops and met many lively
people with innovative ideas. I remember listening to Barney
Young and Michael Rossman relate their experiences with
children in Menlo Park and Berkeley. I also saw Ron Jones
again. During the conference I realized that another person
was attending many of the same workshops. We talked and
I learned that he was involved with preschool age children in
a unique way. He was Gary Barton and his group, located in
the Haight Ashbury area of San Francisco, was called the
Cookie Monster School. Together they planned extensive wil-
derness camping trips and published a weekly newspaper. We
shared ideas that day and later exchanged letters and visits.

As soon as I started organizing Little Room, I began a
detailed journal in which I wrote daily. I kept it for several years. The process helped me express and record my
feelings about the many changes in my life. Looking back in
the journal I noticed that I kept postponing the first day.
Supposedly, a few things were not ready, but actually I was
not ready. The first day did come though and I gathered
courage from a dream of one of the little girls. Chiqui
Moore who was five, told me that morning:

> I dreamed that you gave me and Ori some
> beautiful wings. My wings were blue and
> silver and Ori's wings were yellow and
> gold. You told us we could fly. So we
> put them on and flew up in the sky.

What a wonderful dream and what a good way to begin!

The first week began with Nadja, Augie, Ori, Davi, and Chiqui. They were as varied as their names. Some of the children were quite independent and others clung to dolls, lunch boxes, and blankets from home. The youngest child was almost two and the oldest was five years old. I appreciated the age span because it created a range of needs yet provided the group with opportunities to help each other. For the first few weeks several of the parents stayed part of the time. Also, students from the house dropped in to see what was happening. Not only were there tricycles in front of the building but young children in the bathroom and kids' art in the dining room. Many of those curious students became regular visitors to read stories, make music, or just escape academia. At the end of the first month our group had grown quite comfortable in our Little Room and I looked forward to the times ahead.

In planning the program of Little Room I proceeded carefully. I spent some time reminiscing about my favorite experiences when I was young. I also looked at the activities my daughter and her friends enjoyed together. I had many ideas but chose to wait and plan with the children. Their interests and curiosity soon provided us much to explore and discover. I appreciated beginning that way rather than working from a set curriculum. I felt more comfortable facilitating activities rather than teaching in a traditional sense. I found that our projects, possibly because they were child-centered, were varied and, contrary to the belief that young children have short attention spans, sometimes lasted for days and became quite elaborate.

Having a child-centered rather than a teacher-centered emphasis opened wonderful opportunities. I found that I did not have to be tied to plans and schedules but could be more spontaneous and creative. Our projects were not predetermined but could be developed any number of ways. I also discovered that I could stretch an activity to challenge the growing abilities of some or tailor the same activity to the special needs of another. By staying sensitive to child-initiative, I learned from the group process as well as from individual children. I also gained an awareness that my attention to individuals did not overlook the group as a whole but enhanced it instead.

In addition to group activities, free play became an important part of each day. Using the materials in our Little Room, children were free to play alone or in small groups. I did not become directly involved in their play but watched interactions, relearning the value of peer play and friendship.

Since the first winter was quite rainy I devoted much of my energy to indoor projects. One rain-filled day I pulled out a roll of newsprint from the Palo Alto Times. Everyone eagerly helped me unroll the paper the length of the lounge which was next to our little room. Then one by one I traced seven wiggly children sprawled in many shapes. We spent considerable time tracing, coloring, and cutting out those paper people. Sensing the project was nearing its natural end and knowing the wet

18

weather was persisting, I frantically tried to think of something active. Suddenly I had a vision of children rolled in newsprint. When I told everybody, it took no time before everyone was rolling and paper was flying. We all laughed ourselves silly. Afterward we gathered the newsprint in one large wad and stuffed it into the fireplace. We went to the kitchen and made hot carob and came back to enjoy it in front of a toasty fire. That led into a quiet time in which everyone took turns making up parts of a very long, complicated story. I have often repeated that tracing project in many places and with different groups of children but I will never forget the spontaneity and excitement that first rainy morning.

The Little Room garden was a favorite project because its process seemed to be as rewarding as its products. Our plot was next to the group gardens on campus which were planted by students from the dorms and from Escondido Village. Every few days we would each set out in bare feet and rolled up pants, with a wagon, a wheelbarrow, or small-sized garden tools. The distance seemed short because we worked out an elaborate system concerning whose turn it was to pull or push what when. The first day we prepared the ground by digging and mixing in sand, compost, and manure. Another day we made rows and planted our seeds. Then we transplanted some bright yellow marigolds which we had started in pots back at Little Room. That, according to theory, kept insects away. Last we fenced in our garden with a short wire fence and Calvino De Fillippi and his son Seth brought us foot high sunflowers for the corners. Several students from Ecology House would often come with us on our garden treks. Occasionally other gardeners would give us some of their surplus vegetables. Our salads that winter were delicious. Another year we planted packages of silly seeds which gave us a harvest of a fifty pound pumpkin, yard long cucumbers, and ten foot high sunflowers.

Any time our activities involved food, I could expect eager participation. We did some baking in Ecology House's oven. We also used a blender, a juicer, and an electric frying pan in Little Room. The children learned to prepare snacks using egg beaters, peelers, graters, and butter knives. Together we concocted many things with whole grain flours, honey, dried fruits, nuts, and other nutritious ingredients. During the warmer months we made frozen bars from fruit juice and Tiger's Milk. Those treats were made in small three ounce cups with wooden stirring sticks for handles.

One food project all the children seemed to enjoy was popping corn "the funny way." An electric corn popper without a lid was placed in the center of a cotton sheet with all the children around the edge. As everyone waited for the first kernel to pop we sometimes sang, "Pop Goes the Weasel." Other times a few children would curl their bodies into tight pop corn seed shapes and then fly into the air with the first loud pop. After all the corn had popped out onto the sheet, it was gathered into piles for each child and our snack began.

Once we made pudding for a mid-morning snack. While cleaning the mixing bowl one of the children began finger-painting on the sides. When I saw that wonderful improvisation I quickly made more pudding and we all created delicious pictures on cafeteria trays. That serendipitous experience has since become a part of the regular art program in many schools.

Along with cooking projects I felt that food as a basic need should be an important part of Little Room. For that reason I kept a snack box filled with raisins, fruit, and crackers for times when the group or a particular child was feeling especially hungry.

Many of our activities were not prearranged but spontaneous. We did not visit a fire house because they visited us. The campus fire department came to inspect fire extinguishers and then let us climb on their large, red engine. Another time a Penninsula Creamery truck made a delivery to the kitchen and as a surprise, the driver pulled out yogurt bars for everyone. Occasionally when my car looked a little dusty, we declared it car wash day and proceeded to fill buckets with warm, soapy water. Tricycles, wagons, trucks, dolls, and a few small children, as well as my car, were washed in the process.

In addition to incorporating the immediate environment around us, field trips became an exciting part of Little Room. My Datsun station wagon was affectionately named "Blueberry" and used as the vehicle for our many trips. We visited all of the local parks and established many favorites. Some times we discovered prospective families for our group. At one park I met Jodi Ranuio who immediately decided to send her son and stayed actively involved for the next six years.

Because Little Room was on the Stanford campus there were many places we could walk. Once we had lunch under the umbrellas at Tresidder Student Union. Other times we

visited art and photography exhibits in galleries. The
museums with their marble stairs were wonderful. We
wandered through them seeing antique toys, Indian
artifacts, Rodin sculptures, large canvases with bright
colors, and real mummies. Also there was Hoover Tower.
We took the elevator up many times. We compared views
on clear and foggy days or just looked around. Other
times we visited parents who were students. They showed
us special rocks, fish, and animals which were part of
their department collections. I also checked the Stanford Daily for children's events. Occasionally we
were able to watch puppet shows or dance rehearsals.

One day we walked to the Children's Center of the
Stanford Community to use their outside play equipment.
There I met Eric Remington who was one of the teachers.
He invited us into his room to see his snakes and owl.
When I saw a pair of ducks waddling in and out freely
I knew that his was not just an ordinary class room.
Inside there were also many kinds of animals in tanks
and boxes which the children handled quite naturally.
Eric and I talked about our programs and the things we
hoped to do. We have stayed in touch and our mutual
interest in young children has kept us good friends.

Since the children and I enjoyed being outside in a
natural environment, we took full advantage of Stanford's
vast open space. Lake Lagunita became one of our favorite
places to explore. There we caught polliwogs and kept
them until they matured into frogs, later returning them
to their birth pond. Other times we collected newts,
earthworms, and insects for our terrarium. I learned to
look again at all the things children see so easily. We

also spent some time on the sandy beach building castles
and digging holes. Once we made plaster of paris casts of
our hands and feet in the wet sand. That experiment
proved well worth the effort. Being outdoors with the
children felt special to me.

Back at Little Room, when the weather grew warmer, we
often moved outside into the courtyard. For those days
dress up, play dough, and easel painting became new activities in a changed environment. One week we spent the
entire time outside involved in construction. Each family
brought cardboard boxes in various sizes from regular car-
tons to refrigerator containers. We cut doors and windows,
sculptured tunnels and turrets. I used a staple gun to
attach egg flats, styrofoam, and mailing tubes. The
children made designs on the boxes using felt tip pens
and tempera paint. We glued on wrapping paper, aluminum
foil, and crepe paper streamers. The boxes were trans-
formed into castles, dungeons, caves, and stores. Make-
believe prevailed the whole week and on Friday each child
took home part of the fantasy.

Little Room attracted many visitors; not only families
needing child care, but others just interested in seeing
what was happening. Mike Young and Ron Jones came by one
day. Mike wanted to see my triwall cardboard creations
in action and Ron came with a proposal; would I write a
Little Room article for the next Zephyros Primer? I
eagerly agreed and arranged to see him in a few days.

Ron and I met at his campus office where he worked as
Director of The Student Center for Innovation in Research
in Education, (SCIRE). Unlike most administrative offices
at Stanford his had a box of free kittens in the corner

and a secretary who used caligraphy instead of an IBM
Selectric. Ron showed me some past magazines and then we
walked over to the Design Loft to see the next issue in
various stages of production. There I met George Corey
who was laying out a section. He showed me how photographs were reduced and how the text was pasted up. His
article was a collection of plans for playgrounds constructed from discarded or inexpensive materials. I was impressed with his ideas and began to worry about organizing my
article in the short time that was left. With that intro-
duction, Ron gave me a stack of printers' sheets and an
encouraging smile.

With a little over a week to finish the article I
began frantically writing and called two friends for help.
Both were mothers of children in Little Room. Rosalind
Martins agreed to come in and take photographs and Lea
Honea said she would be happy to make a few sketches. We
all worked quickly and the article was submitted on time.

At the end of April I planned a picnic at my house
because I began to wonder about the summer and Little Room's
future. We had an informal meeting and I was overwhelmed
by the response. Everyone wanted to continue through the
summer and many brought friends who were also interested.
After a week of careful consideration, I decided to expand
our group to ten children with a different parent participating each day. Increasing the number of children also
meant that we would have to find a larger space; Little
Room simply could not accommodate so many. The decision to
move was difficult because I knew I would miss our Little
Room, but somehow I had a good feeling for what seemed to be
ahead. Having the support and appreciation of the parents

made going ahead to another year and another place a whole new adventure. I received a note from Jane Wood, sharing her sentiments. In part she wrote:

> I think this year was a really good one. Sarah comes home everyday babbling about strange things like trucks and ducks and big balloons making noises. It must be all those movies you show from the audio visual department. See you in May!

SECOND YEAR

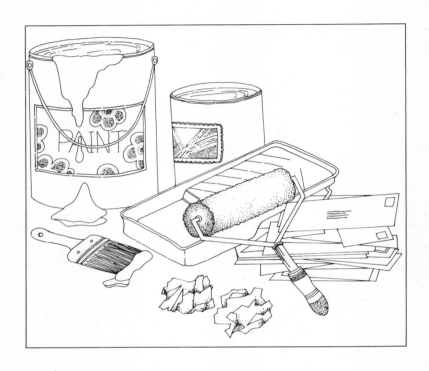

Just as Little Room had been easily found, another
place magically appeared; almost as if a fairy godmother
had some influence. Virginia Debs, a personal friend
with many connections in the community and also director
of Parents' Cooperative Nursery School, suggested I contact
St. Mark's Episcopal Church. With a twinkle in her eye she
described the church's rambling ten acres and the large
park next door. She also mentioned that the rectors were
interested in the issue of child care. Encouraged by her
spirit, I hurried to meet with Colin Campbell and
Dean Underwood. I described Little Room and our need for
more space and also gave them copies of the article I had
written for the Zephyros Primer. My request for a room
was taken to committee and vestry meetings and after a
wait which seemed endless I was given an answer. They
generously offered me a place in their educational building with the condition I protect the church by carrying
insurance and by becoming licensed with the state as a
nursery school. I happily agreed and was given two
sunny rooms and a fenced yard, rent free.

Attending to licensing and other official requirements,
proved to be the focus of the next year and a half. Once
we began I felt Pandora's Box opening. Out sprang an
endless encounter with pure bureaucracy. Not only did I

discover the many facets of state licensing, but additional requirements for a Use Permit with the City of Palo Alto and procedures for nonprofit incorporation for our group so that the church could legally extend space to us and continue its own property tax exempt status. There were also many forms to file for Workmen's Compensation, liability and accident insurance, and a lengthy description for the County Assessor's Office.

Since I can manage details but have never been obsessively compulsive about them, I did not worry about accomplishing everything immediately. I knew the process would take time. To begin I took out insurance and conscientiously notified all the appropriate agencies, waiting to hear from them. Then, knowing that Little Room had run successfully without all that official documentation, I simply returned to the children and let the bureaucracies roll on.

As we moved from our small room at Stanford to a larger area at St. Mark's, I was aware that we could not be a Little Room again. But when the loft was reassembled in the corner and it no longer filled most of the space, I suddenly felt sad. Though we could not be Little Room, I quickly reasoned that like the loft the original spirit of our first small group would continue. For me, the loft served as a connection between Little Room and the beginning of our cooperative. We chose the name "Little People's Co-op" and our group stabilized at ten children with a different parent participating each day. Working with children within their families added an exciting dimension. For me, that beginning felt special.

During that first hot summer we spent most of the time outside. Our yard was filled with long grass and had

a large date palm with fronds that touched the ground. We
moved our wading pool and sand box under it for shade.
We also took many trips. We explored parks from Los
Altos to Fremont. We waded in streams and picked black-
berries. We followed trails and visited farms. Twice a
week we watched Mary Rose's and Lynn's traveling puppet
show. Their puppets recreated wonderful fairy tales.
Also that summer we rode the new Bay Area Rapid Transit
(BART), from Fremont to Richmond. The parents seemed
to enjoy the electric, computer run train as much as the
children.

In July one of the parents, Janet Flegal, asked if
I would be interested in the loan of a computer toy. Her
husband Bob, and his colleagues at Xerox Palo Alto Research
Center were looking for an environment with young children
in which to try out a special learning device. I hesitated,
but was curious.

I went to Xerox and met Radia Perhlman whose advisor,
Seymour Papert, of MIT's Artificial Intelligence Laboratory,
developed the toy turtle. When I first saw the turtle
I wondered at the name because it little resembled its
counterpart in nature, except possibly the shape. Inside
a clear plastic dome was a maze of colored wires and
lights. Radia and Chris Jeffers showed me how to call up
the program by typing in a few lines and explained how
the turtle and button box controls were connected to the
terminal which was linked to a computer via a phone. The
children could easily operate the turtle through the button
box. Each button was marked with a picture symbol command
which would manoeuvre the turtle forward, backward, right,
and left any number of times. Also a light and beeper

could be activated and the turtle's meandering path traced.

I was given a tour of Xerox and shown many of its other "toys." The atmosphere was light with white walls and large windows overlooking the Bay. There were many colored pillows and hanging plants. I was especially impressed by their bean bag-filled lecture room. That became a favorite spot for the children when we returned for visits.

A week later Chris, Bob, and Radia moved the terminal and turtle to our room. The night before the children saw the turtle I decided to give it some character. I attached a green felt tail and feet complete with toes. The face was given expression with bulging Ping-Pong ball eyes attached to springs and suction cups. That first morning the children approached the turtle with caution. Soon however, there was a line of children waiting their turn "to make it go." The turtle stayed with us several months.

Toward the end of the summer local and state agencies began notifying me. In the midst of that Janet Flegal asked if she could help with finances and paper work in place of her co-op time during mornings. I welcomed her and together we formed a united front. We were soon deluged with mail addressed to Ms. Flegal and Ms. Anholt announcing further regulations and requirements. I was not only glad to have Janet's administrative skills but her good-natured support. Many times our business discussions ended in unbelievable laughter.

The first thing Janet and I tackled was the Use Permit issued by the City of Palo Alto. It proved to be a time consuming process. For that permit we paid an

initial fee and then another fee to have several maps of
the church property copied. Next we had to hand-copy from
a thick file, names and addresses of residents within a
200 foot perimeter of the church's ten acres. That list included several apartments and a double row of houses. Then
we had to set up a hearing with the planning department
and address the notices announcing the date of the hearing
to all the residents. After working on that for hours
we wondered what the original fee covered. During
the next few weeks we were visited by the Health Department, Fire Department, and a group filing an environmental impact report. We learned that a Use Permit
could be denied if only one resident had a sufficient
reason for not wanting us to use the property. We
nervously awaited the hearing. The first hearing was
cancelled and rescheduled. The second hearing was also
postponed. Finally, the third hearing actually happened
and was attended by ten parents and a handful of children. There were no residents present. After a few
remarks from the planning commissioner and some formal-
ities we were granted a Use Permit.

     The next thing to reach us by mail was a lengthy
form from the County Assessor's office. In order to use
church property Little People's Co-op needed to show its
nonprofit status. I began researching the process for
incorporation and discovered that the simplest way, at that
time, was to work through a lawyer, spending a considerable
amount of money on fees. By good fortune I talked with
Shira Barnett who was a Zephyros board member. She explained that Zephyros was a nonprofit corporation which had been
set up as an umbrella to cover the innovative, educational

31

projects of several teachers. She suggested I make a pre-
sentation at their next meeting and ask for membership.

A special Zephyros meeting was called where I described
my project and our need for incorporation. A consensus in
favor of my joining was quickly reached. Thus we became
Little People's Co-op, Zephyros Incorporated, and a good
association began.

The last and biggest obstacle in becoming "official"
was obtaining our State Nursery School License. I filed
our application and waited for the infamous unannounced
visit by the licensing representative. Nothing happened
for many months.

The rest of the year unfolded slowly. We moved to
the other end of the building and soon the children,
parents, and I settled into our new room. Sweet potatoes
and avocado seeds were sprouted in glass jars and
placed on the window ledges. Art work was produced and
hung on the walls. Mobiles were constructed and
suspended from the lights. Outside, the playground was
weeded and broken swings were fixed. An abandoned shed
was repaired and painted and then filled with toys. A
parent made a work bench and soon all the little hammers
and saws were put to use. Wood scraps became boats,
planes, and walkie-talkies. Seeds were planted and
vines began covering our cyclone fence. Slowly, Little
People's Co-op began to take on an identity shaped by all
of us. The environment became comfortable and everyone
began feeling close to it. The cooperative spirit ran
high.

In the middle of all that creative activity we came
in direct contact with the church. The contact proved

to be a major confrontation which I learned years later
might have shortened our history. It all began the day
my friend Shira Barnett and I had lunch together. She had
just visited a new toy store with rainbow colored walls.
The colors were so vivid that she asked where they had
been purchased. The manager not only told her but gave
her gallons of half used paint cans from the back room.
She brought back gallon after gallon of red, orange,
yellow, blue, and purple paint. I had never been happy
with the bland colors in our room and had become tired
of trying to cover them with bright posters. The church
had painted our walls an off white, a fleshy salmon pink,
and a beigey brown. The toal effect reminded someone
once of melting Neapolitan ice cream. The walls
were hardly exciting. The next day I asked one of
the rectors if we could paint the room and he said it
seemed okay with him. We started that week. Several
parents came in after school and we began painting the
doors and bookcases a bright red. It looked wonderful.
The next week we started to paint the walls. One room we
alternated between orange and yellow. The other room we
painted blue and purple.

At that point Ray, the custodian who was a good
friend, came running to tell us that our painting was
causing a commotion in the church office. I explained
that I had first asked and that it had seemed all
right. He said the Sunday School teacher who used the
same room on Sunday objected to the red doors. I groaned,
thinking that soon she would also be seeing orange,
yellow, blue, and purple. The rooms were half done with
bits of white, salmon, and beige still showing. I

felt that it would be wise to finish painting quickly so
that the walls would look better. That night a crew of
six dedicated parents finished the two rooms. It was
hard work. The next day the other rector called to
say he was coming to inspect our space because he had
received a number of complaints. I gulped and quickly
moved all the toys back into the room to make it look
less stark. The walls were still wet and the room
smelled of sticky enamel. Having anticipated a difficult morning, I arranged the night before to have a
supportive friend, Adam Honea, help me that morning. He
took care of the children while I talked with the three
men from the church office. They were the two rectors
and the president of the Vestry, who also happened to
be both the husband of the Sunday School teacher and
the Palo Alto Police Chief. I felt very nervous as I
faced two clerical collars and a police badge. I
explained that the paint was good quality and that the
enamel would hold up for years with the kind of use
the room would receive. We talked for a while but the
three men did not say much or look very happy. Finally,
they left.

I quickly called Virginia Debs and she came
to look at the room and loved it. She went to the
church office and diplomatically explained that,
for the first time in years, the room looked like
a learning center. For weeks the custodian kept
me informed about the paint controversy. Feelings
cooled but the incident was never totally resolved or
forgotten. Five years later Rector Colin Campbell still
half joked with me about "Uni's paint job."

Just after the paint incident we had another confrontation, this time with the State Department of Health about our license. Janet and I prepared ourselves for our last great adventure in officialdom. That process proved to be very frustrating and at times almost ridiculous. After receiving notice from the licensing division we sent away to Sacramento for a weighty booklet called Title XXII. It contained everything necessary for a license. With great amazement we skimmed through its 691 pages of rules and regulations. It dealt with requirements for square footage indoors and outdoors per child, percentage of windows to walls, number of doors and toilets, as well as miniscule details concerning fencing, playground surfaces, drinking fountain heights, and food provisions. Title XXII devoted pages to types of programs, curriculum, equipment as well as qualifications of the staff in terms of educational degrees, course units, and pre-school related work experience.

To begin we sent in maps, architectural drawings, finger prints, resumes, letters, and transcripts. They sent us additional forms and requests for more information. The great paper shuffle began. Soon they learned that we were operating quite openly without a license and the paper shuffle made way for unending phone calls and unannounced visits. We then met our licensing representative and quickly learned she had a reputation for the strictest interpretation of the regulations in the history of her department.

I realized at that point that even with a BA in social psychology and some courses in education, I needed some preschool program units. I quickly enrolled at De Anza College and once a week attended a morning, afternoon, and evening laboratory class. That continued for a semester while someone worked one morning a week for me. For the most part the classes were very basic and quite boring. The best part was meeting other people in the class who were in similar situations as myself. Often a group of us would pass notes to break the monotony. I felt as if I was in high school again. Those people included Eric Remington whom I met the year before at the Children's Center at Stanford, Mona Key who directed the Jewish Community Center Nursery School, and Helen Pillsbury who later taught preschool classes at De Anza College and Greenmeadows Nursery School. We became close as we car pooled to mandatory classes. Later we visited each other at our own programs.

After taking those courses I was informed by the licensing representative that I was one administrative course short of being a qualified director. Even though I was currently enrolled in an administration and supervision class, I soon received an official notice declaring that our program must "cease and desist."

I called a parent meeting and we discussed the matter. The seriousness of it gave way to lighthearted joking as we decided to send letters and petitions to our licensing representative, her supervisor, and Sacramento. The support from the letters was wonderful. Parents used full names, letterhead stationery, and degrees after their names if they had any. Some described the quality of the program. Others wrote about their need for child care. I especially enjoyed

Kit Bricca's letter. It was written in a true organizer's style with the content stressing the narrowness of the interpretation of the regulations and the state's usual interference with something positive. He wrote that we would contact local organizations, newspapers, and radio stations if the department tried to close us down. All those letters as well as pictures and notes from the children were sent.

A month later we were asked to a meeting with our licensing representative in her office. That night before I role played the impending meeting with my friends Adam Honea and Bill Giordano. It was helpful and soothed my nervous energy. The next day Janet and I drove to the State Department of Health in San Jose. Janet was amazed as I arranged my chair on the same side of the desk as the licensing representative and proposed a plan. Virginia Debs and I had prearranged that she could "supervise" me and act as official director for a month until my administration class was over. She would do so on a daily basis by scheduling her own parent conferences in our building. Our representative accepted that arrangement on the condition Virginia's fingerprints and transcripts be on file. Janet and I happily agreed and our little place did not "cease and desist."

Two years later and long after we were properly licensed, that same licensing representative visited on her annual unannounced inspection. After she noted on her yellow sheet that our playground needed weeding and one tricycle was broken, she revealed to me that she would soon be leaving her job with the state. She told me that she hoped to open a children's center that

37

would be large and equipped with the latest in child development. She also said the staff would not be paid low hourly wages but given a salary equivalent to public school teachers. Then she asked me if I would consider the position of director. I looked at her speechlessly. She smiled and gave me her card saying, "Think about it."

THIRD YEAR

Pooh's first idea was that they should dig a Very Deep Pit, and then the Heffalump would come along and fall into the Pit, and --

"Why?" said Piglet.

"Why what?" said Pooh.

"Why would he fall in?"

Pooh rubbed his nose with his paw, and said that the Heffalump might be walking along, humming a little song, and looking up at the sky, wondering if it would rain, and so he wouldn't see the Very Deep Pit until he was half-way down, when it would be too late.

Piglet said that this was a very good Trap, but supposing it were raining already?

Pooh rubbed his nose again, and said that he hadn't thought of that. And then he brightened up, and said that, if it were raining already, the Heffalump would be looking at the sky wondering if it would clear up, and so he wouldn't see the Very Deep Pit until he was half-way down. . . . When it would be too late.

Piglet said that, now that this point had been explained, he thought it was a Cunning Trap.

Pooh was very proud when he heard this, and he felt that the Heffalump was as good as caught already, but there was just one other thing which had to be thought about, and it was this. Where should they dig the Very Deep Pit?

Piglet said that the best place would be
somewhere where a Heffalump was, just before
he fell into it, only about a foot farther on.
"But then he would see us digging it," said
Pooh.
"Not if he was looking at the sky."
"He would Suspect," said Pooh, "If he
happened to look down." He thought for
a long time and then added sadly, "It
isn't as easy as I thought. I suppose
that's why Heffalumps hardly ever get
caught.
"That must be it," said Piglet.

At the bottom of parent newsletters I serialized the
Heffalump chapter from Winnie the Pooh. Besides the usual
messages found in dittoed newsletters, each issue contained
the next installment of Pooh's and Piglet's adventures. I
loved the story and thought to myself that the children and
I could also pursue that fantasy. Our chances of finding a
Heffalump were probably as good as Pooh's and Piglet's, and
meanwhile, what a wonderful time we could have. At the
beginning of that third year we changed our name and
officially became "Heffalump."

After our previous exposure to licenses, permits, and
inspections, the year felt calm and creative. In the fall
handbook I wrote with a sigh of relief:

I feel a long struggle is over
and now chances of survival are
good! Heffalumps, after all, are
nice things to have around.

During the year I was pleased with the parents. The
majority had experience with cooperatives and communities

42

which made organizing Heffalump around those ideals a joy. Many had been active in the antiwar movement and involved with such groups as the American Friends' Service Committee, the Institute for the Study of Non-violence, the United Farm Workers of America, Child Care Now, the Tenants' Union, food cooperatives, and later the Briarpatch Market. The year was characterized by break-fast planning sessions convening at seven o'clock with as many as ten participants. It was also a year of increased parent involvement, an afternoon program, work days, and fund raising.

In working with the children and their parents together, I hoped to create a cohesive group. A group in which each child's needs were met and where parents could learn more about young children and understand their own child better within that setting. I found it important to get to know each parent well and build rapport. From those efforts a good relationship was formed in which parents were not "helpers" but partners in our cooperative. Parent skills and interests often became spring boards for our adventures, including them in a real and meaningful way.

Parent involvement contributed substantially to our activities. I also tried to stay informed of local events and resources in the community. With that approach, we enjoyed a full program which was not bound by the walls of our building or confined by a set curriculum. Some days were low-keyed with familiar activities. Others were charged with energy and exploration. I loved discovering new things with the children and found that when we were all challenged the results were exciting.

One activity I will always remember is our first bus trip. In the early fall I read about a new transportation plan for Santa Clara County. It was an innovative experiment called Dial-a-Bus and proved to be just what it claimed. A computer system organized bus routes from telephone requests. The day before Dial-a-Bus went into effect I spent considerable time on the phone. Finally I got through and made an appointment for our group stating our address, destination, and approximate times for the round trip. The next morning Dial-a-Bus drove into the parking lot and picked up thirteen little children and four adults. The driver gave everyone paper transfers punched full of holes. She dropped us off at a park in Mountain View and returned two hours later for our return. It was an exciting journey as we zigzagged through back streets picking up riders at their homes. Some of the children had never been on a bus before. A few discovered the overhead wire which signals a stop. Others kept their noses pressed against the windows. The whole odyssey was recorded by Sara Wood-Smith with her movie camera. The total cost of the trip was fifty cents for each adult. For Heffalump Dial-a-Bus was a huge success, but it was soon discontinued by the county for cost inefficiency.

Sara later returned with her movie camera and we staged silent melodramas with the children. Everyone dressed in costumes from the dress up basket and climbed in and out of tunnels, sheds, parachutes, and tires. The camera was stopped and started as different children took their places. After it was developed we

saw a hilarious movie. One funny scene showed dozens
of children coming out of a stack of large tires much
in the style of circus clowns piling out of a little
car. Those movies were shown again and again at
Heffalump and parent gatherings.

The previous year Bill Scarvie, a parent of two
Heffalumpers, brought a video camera and we were able
to see ourselves on a television. The children became
excited and started humming the themes from Zoom and
Sesame Street. Some thought they would see themselves
next to Big Bird. Bill made tapes of the children and
played them back to an entranced audience. The porta-
pak camera was light enough so that with a little help
some of the older children could make their own shows.
It was interesting to see what things they chose for
subjects and how they captured them. I remember one
child taping two children rolling a ball between
them. Unlike an adult who might focus in on each
child's face as he or she caught the ball, that child
very carefully followed only the ball back and forth and
back again. For me, that perspective was refreshing.

Another activity which quickly became a weekly
outing was trekking through Foothills Park. Only
fifteen minutes from Heffalump, this 1400 acre park
provided us with a vista hill, a lake, trails, meadows,
and an interpretative center. Foothills is nestled in
the Coast Range Mountains and looks out over the Bay
from San Francisco across to Mt. Diablo and Mt.
Hamilton and south to San Jose. There we spent many
happy days looking for newts, banana slugs, and gold
back ferns. Sometimes we hiked to the island playing

45

trolls and goats on the bridge. Other times we fed
the ducks stale bread from a local bakery or sailed
handmade boats. During the windy spring months we
flew dragon and bat kites.

Our favorite spot was the bay laurel tree. It
had many different trunks that grew out of the side of
a steep embankment. Upon first seeing it I was
reminded of Tolkien's description of the Ent trees in
the Lord of the Rings trilogy. Like the Ent wives the
tree had a very maternal aspect, enhanced by a dozen
children climbing in and over and around its trunks and
limbs. The children spent many hours climbing and sliding
and making up games. Out of the dust and stirring leaves
arose a most wonderful bay tree smell. The sunlight
filtered through the thick foliage with a soft green light
that made lacy patterns on the ground. In spite of the
noise an occasional deer would wander over and seem
to watch. At the end of our play out came many dirty
little children with the seat of their pants black.
Parents soon learned that the level of fun seemed to be
in direct proportion to the amount of soil on their
children's clothes and began sending their little ones to
Heffalump in washable jeans and overalls.

In the middle of the year some of the parents voiced a
need for an afternoon program as many of them returned to
school or found part-time employment. Our four hour morning program was too short for them. We had several meetings
and decided to add a four hour afternoon session. Jodi
Ranuio and Patti Bricca, both with children in Heffalump,
and Shira Barnett, offered to work in the new program. In
the beginning there were sometimes only two or three child-

ren but soon the afternoon began to stabilize around five. The afternoon session was a great addition to Heffalump and welcomed by families which needed all day care. The three women tenaciously held the program together until the summer when Anne Branch joined us and organized all the sessions. From its small beginnings the afternoon soon came into its own. Patti went on to form a school based on co-counseling principles while Jodi and Shira returned to their studies.

During that year, work days became an important part of Heffalump. In addition to the time parents spent with the children they also participated in a bimonthly work-day or took a task home. That enabled us to maintain our space and add new materials to the environment. The parent group also began making plans for a wooden play structure in a spot overgrown with thistles. Parent Ken Artunian, a professional architect and landscaper, drew up formal blueprints and submitted them to the church. After committee consideration the project was approved for the following year.

Since Heffalump's beginning, tuition had been kept low with the budget extending only a little beyond staff's salaries. We operated on a narrow margin and relied heavily on parent co-op time, work days, and the donation of supplies. In order to build up our reserves and cover rising costs we decided to try fund raising on a small scale. When we began I remembered a poster I had once seen in an inner city school: "It will be a great day when our schools get all the money they need, and the Navy has to hold a bake sale to buy a ship."

Our first attempt was a showing of the Red Balloon

and our Heffalump produced movie. We felt the films would net us some money and also publicize our program. Since the movies and projector were free, as well as the meeting hall, refreshments, and our labor, we looked forward to a high return with a minimum amount of effort.

On that Saturday morning several parents set up the hall. The screen, chairs, and snack table were arranged and the projector was threaded. To everyone's horror, the projector would not work. With only an hour before the first showing, they frantically began looking for another.

Meanwhile, I was at Woolworth's helping the manager inflate the balloons he had donated. After struggling over an hour with those slippery balloons, I think he began to regret his generosity. He helped me load them in my car. After I squeezed behind the wheel he carefully pushed in a few extra through a side window. Every square inch of my car was solidly packed with helium filled balloons. Fortunately I had a balloon's worth of open space in front of me in order to see. However, I soon found that I had to fight the shifting balloons to keep that space. As I navigated the car I fantasized that at any moment the car might slowly start rising above the pavement. When I reached the hall I began honking the horn, calling for help. A few people came running. They all began laughing, as the balloons had been kept as a surprise.

By that time another projector had been found and everything was ready. With the balloons we walked into the darkened hall filled with restless children.

The movies were wonderful. We ran out of balloons. And our first fund raiser was a success!

FOURTH YEAR

Having Ori with me each day, from the beginning of Little Room, was special. I appreciated being able to combine mothering and working simultaneously. That unique arrangement enabled me to be a full-time mother while earning an income and pursuing professional skills. Those roles enhanced each other as they became entwined. I never had to deny my motherhood and sometimes felt as if I also was the mother of a large family. At other moments I experienced the excitement of discovering professional directions for myself.

The fourth year was a turning point as Ori left Heffalump to begin kindergarten. On that day in early September, together with many other parents, I saw myself letting go of a baby who had become a young child. As I watched Ori skip happily into her new classroom, I knew that our previous years together had been just right.

I returned to Heffalump with renewed energy and readied myself for one of the most challenging years. The program expanded to its largest enrollment with four full-time staff members. I was joined in the morning by Ruth Vavuris. Ann Branch, who ran the afternoon session during the summer, stayed and developed a close-knit after school kindergarten program. She worked in the afternoon with Dan Gurney who had had much experience with preschool age children. Later in the year Mary Anne Fischer, a Stanford student, teamed with Dan part-time. With a morning session and a combined after kindergarten and preschool afternoon program, Heffalump lumped ahead at full capacity with its first waiting list.

After beginning we noticed that many of the families were unfamiliar with cooperatives. Because of an increased enrollment and a greater need for parent involvement, we quickly defined the nature of Heffalump, a cooperative. That seemed to be helpful for those parents and also for others who were simply resistant to participating. After expectations were clearly stated I was amazed at how soon a community feeling developed. Involvement varied from family to family yet the required minimum always seemed to be met. In fact, families who at first had the most difficulty complying with cooperative requirements, eventually grew to be some of the strongest supporters of Heffalump. Seeing that, I felt relieved that my initial hard-nosed position had not been in vain.

During the first few days Ruth and I found that many of the children lacked a certain social awareness. Their play was constantly interrupted with hitting and grabbing. Since many were young and had never been a part of a group, the need for careful intervention was essential.

To begin we firmly told everyone that we would not allow aggressive behavior but instead we would help them to get along better with each other. We also enlisted their help toward making it a joint effort. Within the program we added more structure, hoping to promote a greater sense of security and predictability. New games and special activities were incorporated to encourage cooperation rather than competition.

With some children we had to work more closely as their negative behavior was repeated again and again.

When their aggression toward others broke loose we had to actively intervene, setting firm limits and often holding them until they were in better control. After emotions cooled we explored the feelings of all the children involved in the incidents. Everyone was encouraged to accept their anger, sadness, or frustration. We wanted to help them express whatever it was that they had experienced, appropriately in words rather than with actions which might hurt another. That intervention and exploratory process was demanding but not without rewards. Soon it could be heard in play, from even the youngest, "Use words, don't hit."

The problem of aggression was not quickly solved. For some, play without fighting was a difficult notion to grasp. Ruth and I tenaciously worked with both groups and individuals using a style which was firm yet gentle. We often saw patterns which led to stressful situations and were careful to restructure those times. In their place we arranged positive experiences. After dealing with negative behavior for some time, we were pleased when changes began to occur.

Because of the high energy level of our group, Ruth and I did not have time to develop a method of working together. Instead we intuitively leaped into action and formed a strong team. We were each supportive of the other and our impromptu strategies proved, in the long run, quite effective. We shared observations and ideas in an approach that relied on constant communication throughout the mornings. I enjoyed working with Ruth and felt our individual personalities and interests were complementary. I appreciated Ruth's ability and willingness to persist through some trying moments. Our group did eventually settle down; respect for each other grew as friendships developed and hugs replaced hitting. The first important steps had been taken and I looked forward to an exciting year.

The year was filled with fairy tales, plays, movies, and meeting time for the children. It was also another year of continued parent involvement in which a play structure was completed, converting a thistle patch into a lush grassy area. One parent made a large wooden sign for the entrance and designed Heffalump tee-shirts. It was a full and happy year.

A high point of the year for me, was using fairy tales with child-centered plays. Since both fairy tales and plays had been a significant part of my childhood, it seemed a natural combination to try a Heffalump.

Today, fairy tales have often been left on the shelf because many adults are hesitant about giants' gruesome threats and other such elements. Much of contemporary children's literature presents only the good side of life with an absence of struggle involving violence, aggression, and evil forces. Even when modern stories use the ancient motifs of the fairy tale, the questionable parts are often rewritten so that trolls only elicit laughter and monsters only eat cookies. Super heroes like batman and spiderman replace the young, innocent child in fairy tales who had to overcome adversities and trials to become a hero in his or her own right. I feel children can identify better with heroes who are like themselves, without capes or nets, but are put to great tests; such as the little girl who, through a series of trials frees her seven brothers, or like Jack, who out-wits

the giant and regains his family's wealth. I remember once
hearing, Anna Meyer, skipping along satirizing the giant's
chant about the blood of an English man. She, like Jack,
had overcome the giant's awesomeness with her own verse:

> Fe, Fi, Fo, Fum.
> I smell the blood of an
> English muffin.

Bruno Bettelheim, a well-known child psychoanalyst,
has written about fairy tales. He feels that stories speak
to the children through the realistic and magical material
within each. Fairy tales seem to tell about the human
situation by expressing both good and evil. He believes
that children can then better accept those qualities in
themselves and others. He is convinced that children are
given answers in symbolic form to questions that need
answering, leading towards growth and maturity.

In my involvement, both with the children at Heffalump
and previously with severely disturbed school age children,
I have felt the powerful impact of the fairy tale. Books
which were reread by popular demand were often not the
beautifully illustrated story books, but fairy tale volumes
which were many times long and involved, and had few pictures. The words alone carried the emotion. The story
seemed to leap from the page and soon was acted out
informally among the children.

At Heffalump I watched these small spontaneous plays
and encouraged groups to work cooperatively on larger plays
with audiences and casts. The plays were repeated again and
again so that everyone could be as many characters as he or
she wished. As our plays became big productions, the
excitement ran high and the attention was intense. Lunch, I

found, was about the only thing that could interrupt our performances.

I discovered that those fairy tale based plays were extremely important. Besides the sheer enjoyment they provided, I saw the plays affecting many children's personal development. The plays allowed some to express themselves in an entirely different way. For others they permitted a release of feeling that had been repressed. The children could see the consequences of aggressive actions and, through role playing, understood the emotions underlying certain situations. The first play we produced was "The Three Billy Goats Gruff." Everyone had the opportunity to be a mean and threatening troll, a scared little baby goat, and a powerful, conquering big goat. Characterization needed no encouragement and within the play context, true cooperation occurred. After using the plays for a short while I began to see children who had difficulty relating with others, change. They began to watch things happening around them with new, inquisitive eyes. Many seemed happier as they became better able to express themselves in their play. The changes which I saw I attribute both to the medium of the play and to the enchanting and magical qualities of the fairy tales.

Throughout the year plays were performed as much as twice a week. We began with simple stories and progressed to ones with many characters. In "Jack and the Bean Stalk" the children not only played the parts of Jack and the giant, but also the golden egg and the magic beans. Our dramatics became very creative. Parents Whitney and Dirk Van Nouhuys both came several times to videotape our plays. The children loved seeing themselves, and families who missed live performances had the opportunity to watch them on tape.

Another addition for Heffalump were movies. Ruth rented a projector from a parochial school and reserved films at a public library. That enabled us to show several movies a week. Some were produced by the Canadian Film Boards, others by European film companies, and many from the Disney animal series. Several were children-made productions. Movie time was also a good excuse to make popcorn and sell pretend tickets.

"Meeting" was a third new addition. Ruth and I created that group time to settle a high activity level and also to provide a focus for the morning. In the beginning the children were too restless to sit and listen. The first meeting lasted several minutes. Soon however, with colorful carpet squares arranged in a circle to sit upon, and an occasional song with the guitar and Autoharp as an opening, the group began to enjoy that daily occurrence. Gradually the length of Meeting increased. It became a place to share a feeling or show something brought from home. Many times we planned trips or parties or talked about a child who would be leaving Heffalump or prepared the group for a new child. Meeting became a valuable experience for most of the children. For some it provided an opportunity to talk. Others participated by listening. It seemed to create a feeling of closeness within the group. Some children were disappointed if it was time to go home and we had not had a meeting. Just as their parents had special meetings, our meeting time seemed to take on that same importance.

The parent group that fourth year was actively involved in Heffalump. Ken Artunian organized everyone

around the construction of the play structure. After
receiving church approval for his design we also arranged to
deduct the cost of materials and labor from the rent which
we had just begun to pay. With those details arranged well
in advance, unlike the painting episode of the second year,
we proceeded with confidence.

The collective experience of our building crew was
impressive. We had two union carpenters, a Palo Alto city
planner, a senior planner at Stanford, an architect, and a
landscape designer. With that expertise and the hard work
of others, we were able to complete the project in three
weekends. We excavated the area, installed an irrigation
system, built the structure, filled the sand area, laid sod,
and planted birch trees. Uldis Nollendorfs arranged for the
use of a Caterpillar and the donation of several cubic yards
of sand. Ken worked many hours and was able to purchase
materials at cost. For the whole project we spent about six
hundred dollars and were able to subtract another four hundred dollars of donated labor from our rent to the church.

The children excitedly watched the progress from week
to week. When it was finished, field trips were postponed
and activities in other areas stopped. Everything happened
around the structure. Even meetings were held on the deck.
That was when we decided that "play-structure" was a rather
unimaginative name and spent one entire meeting thinking of
a new one. When someone quietly suggested "Mouse House,"
all the children immediately squeaked their consensus.
Mouse House it became.

Next to the fence we planted pole beans, sweet peas,
and sunflowers that grew ten feet high. It became a
pleasant place and the thistle patch was soon a faded

memory. By chance a formally dressed woman from the church
wandered over and gasped, "It looks like the Garden of
Eden!" I smiled and thought to myself that she was right,
especially on a hot day when all our naked little children
were running through the sprinklers.

While many parents participated in groups on work
days, I especially appreciated individual projects. Sue
Brown arrived one morning with a baby on her hip and a sign
under her other arm. As a surprise she created a wonderful
wooden sign to hang outside our door. In large letters it
spelled Heffalump between flowers, trees, and forest
animals. Suspended from the sign was a cut-out Pooh Bear.
Sue, who is a professional illustrator, also designed
delightful tee-shirts. On a light blue shirt a fluff white
cloud floated in the shape of the word Heffalump. At the
bottom edge Pooh attempted to rope the cloud. With a little
help from a crow the lasso seemed to catch. That design was
reprinted on posters, stationery, sign-up sheets, and
became our unofficial logo.

During the fourth year, the afternoon session became a
vital part of Heffalump. Dan Gurney ran the preschool program which met the needs of the children who stayed all day.
Usually he arrived on his ten-speed bicycle at one o'clock
and often pulled a magic trick from his back pack. The children loved him and he genuinely enjoyed being with them. Dan
seemed to fill the need some of the children had for an adult
male as many of them were cared for by single, working
mothers. By providing that role model, I know, Dan sometimes
felt drained. Mary Ann Fisher joined him several times a
week and together they created a nurturing environment.

Anne Branch also met in the afternoon with her small group of kindergartners. At lunch time she began a caravan from school to school, picking up children and packing them in her pumpkin-colored Volvo. Her route extended from Mountain View to Menlo Park. During the year her group took unusual field trips and conducted elaborate science experiments. Anne enjoyed the older children and her group grew close as over half of them had been with Heffalump since the first year.

During that year I appreciated Dan's and Anne's dedication and hard work. The helped me realize the staff's need for more communication. They felt that the afternoon session was disconnected from Heffalump because there were no co-oping parents and because there was no continuity with the morning's activites. To look at those problems closer we increased our staff meetings to once a week and began informal potlucks at each others' homes. We discussed changes and ways of increasing support for the afternoon. The idea of rotating staff members between the two sessions was suggested but not used then because of other commitments and work schedules. Many of the ideas coming out of those meetings were used in following years. I learned much from everyone and our sessions together created more solidarity. For me the growth of Heffalump had been fast and many times I felt I was not prepared to deal with all the new responsibilities of being a director. Nevertheless, working together were were better able to meet the needs of the children and parents as our own needs as a staff were explored and understood.

Toward the end of the year Ruth happily told me her plans to marry a long time friend. Since that meant a move from the area we began to look for someone to take her place and to prepare the children for her leaving. We did not have to look long for we found a qualified person who also happened to be Ruth's older sister, Kay. I liked Kay immediately and she very much wanted to be a part of Heffalump. Both sisters worked together to ease a transition and on Ruth's last day we had a party. After all the children had left, I remember Heffalump becoming very quiet. Ruth and I said good-bye with a hug knowing that words could not express what we had shared. We groped for something funny to say but tear and laughter were about all we could manage.

The day after Ruth's wedding, Kay came with a basket of goodies left from the celebration. With the children we had another reception. They happily ate small sandwiches and drank sparkling apple cider from plastic champagne glasses. We then toasted Ruth's marriage and welcomed Kay to Heffalump.

FIFTH YEAR

Heffalump's fifth year brimmed with energy and creativity and also felt quite comfortable. Heffalump had reached a new maturity. In September Peter Wing joined Kay Vavuris and me. Together we reviewed the past years and built upon them with our collective experience. The blending of ideas seemed to enrich the program. Also, many of the administrative details which I found preoccupying were shared among us. We worked well together. In order to know each other better we met regularly and planned occasional day trips to the ocean or woods on weekends.

Organizationally, Heffalump reached its prime. Kay and I enlarged the parent handbook of the previous years and improved other areas of communication. We continued the weekly newsletter and posted a daily journal. Bulletin boards were reorganized and charts were devised to record parent participation. Also, conferences were held with interested parents. With logistical matters well under control, our attention turned toward the children.

We began with a diverse group. Many had been at Heffalump for a while. They played well together and other new children entered that group easily. We also had a few children who had difficulty adjusting. They seemed fearful and anxious and had a hard time interacting positively with the others. In addition,

on a part-time basis, we "mainstreamed" or integrated
children with emotional problems into our program
from a day treatment center. We made those arrange-
ments through the children's parents and special
education teachers at Penninsula Children's Center.
Understanding and working with those exceptional
children within the larger group provided many new
challenges. I looked forward to having such a
varied group and felt confident that our program
could provide for multiple needs.

With an emphasis on special needs, Kay, Peter,
and I spent our staff meetings discussing ways to
balance the entire group. Because Heffalump was
small and had a low ratio of children to adults
we were able to focus on individuals. We found that
our basic program needed only slight modifications
to deal with some children's problems of loss of
control. We prepared ourselves for providing structure and setting definite limits. In some situations
we had to temporarily remove a child from the group.
That intervention was comforting to the child as well
as for the others. Our ability to protect individuals
and the group seemed to promote the security needed
so that social skills could be learned.

With our firmness I was delighted to find that
gentle affection had a similar effect. The results of
hugs and physical touch were wonderful and immediate.
They created an atmosphere of trust in which a problem
could often be further explored with words. Much of
our children's physical aggressiveness seemed to be
asking for positive physical contact, be it soft or

restraining. I remember many times in the middle of some distant commotion, suddenly feeling a little one dive for my lap. The child was usually the instigator of the trouble looking for instant reassurance and help. The warmth of the closeness seemed to provide him or her with the acceptance needed to look at the problem and work out a solution. In dealing with conflict through limits, acceptance and affection became important ingredients.

Looking back and evaluating our experience at Heffalump in combining children with a wide range of abilities and adjustments, I would not hesitate to do it again. I feel everyone benefited. Many of the children gained a broader acceptance for others who were noticeably different from themselves and learned new ways of interaction. The children from the treatment program became a vital part of Heffalump. As they began using newly learned social skills, they experienced the joy of being included. The special education teachers made contact with children developing normally and began to see their own students in perspective. Away from the treatment center and in the Heffalump environment, their children were seen with behavioral problems yet also with many positive and emerging strengths. The co-oping parents, staff, and I learned a tremendous amount from all our Heffalumpers.

For our active children we planned structured activities. However, knowing that that alone was confining for both the children and us, we made use of our ten acres and took extensive field trips.

Structure and space, a seeming contradiction, proved
to be a complementary and successful combination.

With our energetic children, in a period of hot
weather and continued drought, we planned daily
outings. Some were simple; a short walk to a nearby
park. Others were elaborate, involving preparation
for an all-morning expedition. Kay and I both had a
strong interest in exploring the natural environment.
Having studied biology and natural history, Kay
shared wonderful stories about native plants and animals. As we hiked along a trail I loved watching the
children make small discoveries. Our trips seemed to
refresh everyone and gave us new experiences in which
we saw everything differently and each other better.

One of our trips was a monthly, dry creek hike.
It began in the San Franciquito Creek behind Children's
Hospital at Stanford. There among the jungle-like
growth of flaming orange sumac and twisting vines,
we climbed down an embankment to a dry, cracked creek
bed. For a mile we navigated its winding course and
found many interesting treasures: smooth glass,
unusual stones, buckeyes, bald tennis balls, and
abandoned shopping carts. Every strange plant,
footprint, or animal track was carefully inspected.
Occasionally we collected things to bring back for a
collage. Other times those things were forgotten
as the children slid down steep, dusty banks on
little bottoms.

Other trips included visits to some of our
families homes. We scheduled regular trips to the
Jeavons' and Artunians' homesteads. Those amazing

66

places exist within the city limits of Palo Alto.
At Heather Jeavon's house we ate from a greenhouse,
fed baby goats, and jumped into huge piles of straw.
Another fun place to visit was the Artunian farm.
Their one acre is carefully laid out with a garden,
orchard, chicken coop, horse corral, milking barn,
and play area. We went often to feed the chickens,
search for eggs, and brush the horses. Once we made
delicious ice cream from the cow's rich cream. Shortly
after that I found myself returning to do the Sunday
night milking in exchange for a gallon of fresh milk.

What had been occasional outings to Foothills Park
in the past soon became an institution. Every Friday
morning we left Heffalump promptly at 9:30 and returned
at one. We hiked all the paths in the park except the
13 mile long Los Trancos Trail. The Fern Walk took us
through a woodland of ferns and hanging moss. As we
hiked the trail we crossed a meandering stream over a
series of seven bridges. Each time we stopped and
searched for a troll or gnome beneath, but only found
traces of them. Other trails took us through oak, bay,
and redwood forests to open meadows filled with deer
and native grasses. My favorite paths climbed up ridges
into the high chaparral. There we found wild flowers
and lizards and viewed miles of rolling hills and the
San Francisco Bay below.

Many times a narrow trail requiring a single file
line could not accommodate our energetic group. On
those days we fed ducks from the island, flew kites on
top of the hill, or explored streams for creatures. We
often returned to Heffalump with tadpoles for our

aquarium or newts, slugs, and snails for the terrarium.
In the early spring we felt the soft pussywillow, made
plaster of paris prints of deer tracks, ate miner's
lettuce, and went on shaggy lion hunts. At Foothills
Park we never were at a loss for things to do.

Working together with Kay every morning was a
unique experience. Like her favorite plant, the
sunflower, she exuded warmth and energy. Also, being
a bit mischievious, she was called Kay the bluejay by
the children. They felt her gentle spirit as she sang
with her guitar or nursed little birds back to health.
Being a part of Wild Life Rescue she often came to
Heffalump with small birds. The children learned to
feed them when their peeps became loud and constant.
Even the most active children would sit quietly, totally
involved. After the birds recuperated we all helped
release them. Through Kay, the children grew to love
those small creatures and with that experience, gained
a respect for living things.

In addition to the many animals Kay cared for we
came to know other animals. We had a pair of rats
who were quite prolific and an outside hutch filled
with soft bunnies. Eric Remington visited occasionally
with his oppossum, Blossom. He also brought gifts of
alligator lizards and luna moths still in their cocoons.
The year was filled with animals as we visited horse
ranches, large farms, and petting zoos.

While reading my mail around the middle of the
year, I came across an announcement for an innovative
program at California State University at Sonoma. It
offered a master's degree in early childhood and

special education. I was intrigued because it was designed for people who were currently teaching and could
use their present positions as part of the required
field experience. After a few phone calls I left three
days later for the Northern California campus. After
a required three weeks at Sonoma State, I attended the
rest of the weekly lectures in Berkeley and Fremont.
Monthly symposiums were held on weekends and field
work was fulfilled at various agencies around the Bay
Area. I continued with the program for two years and
eventually finished the degree.

I gained many new insights from the graduate
program. Through it I met creative people in the field
of child development and was exposed to issues, some
social, theoretical, practical, or academic. The
combination of the degree program and my work at
Heffalump with children with special needs was personally
stimulating. I began to realize then that my involvement with children felt right. My desire to work more
closely, particularly with children experiencing
difficulties, became stronger. My interest was not
just to facilitate their educational development
through a teaching relationship, but to nurture their
social and emotional adjustment. To achieve that goal
I decided then that I wanted to continue my professional
growth, perhaps in the field of clinical psychology or
social work. I made a decision to make my next year at
Heffalump my last so that I could follow those new
directions. My decision was made quietly so that I
could use my sixth year to define it further. Also,
wanting Heffalump to continue, I felt the need to

create a transition. The transition, I knew then, was
as much for Heffalump as myself. I felt my leaving
would not be easy.

Toward the end of the year Kay decided to go back
to school. She was interested in finishing a degree
in environmental education. It was hard to see her
leave because I had enjoyed working with her, yet I
could understand her desire to finish school. As a
last project together we planned Heffalump's first
overnight camping trip at Foothills Park for all the
families. We thought it would be a good way to end a
special year.

On a Friday night over 60 people gathered for
an eventful night of camping. Tents were pitched
and a potluck dinner was shared. Later, around an
evening campfire children and parents made up impromptu
skits and sang songs to guitar and bass fiddle. Kay
was presented a silver heart necklace as we reminisced.
As the night wore on and shadows danced on tall trees,
little ones were tucked in warm sleeping bags inside
tents. Parents returned to the fire to sing and talk.
It had been a good year.

Long after the fire had burned down and everyone
was asleep, around two a.m., in the middle of a third
year of drought, the sky suddenly opened. It began to
rain and rained steadily for hours. Several tents were
flooded and people scurried to cars and other tents on
higher ground. Some felt that the dirt road leading out
and up a steep hill would be impassable in the morning.
In the dark they attempted to leave but slid back down
the hill. Others sank in mud up to their wheel axles.

The next morning we all ate a soggy breakfast and laughed about the wonderful rain we had not seen for so long. It was still drizzling as we pushed cars and vans out of the heavy mud. Some of us with wet clothes went to fish in the lake, knowing it was the best time for nibbles.

SIXTH YEAR

My last year at Heffalump evoked within me many
feelings. Sadness over leaving was often balanced by eager
anticipation for the future. Knowing that I would only be
there that last year made it very different from all the
others and helped me savor some moments with a certain
nostalgia. I also released Heffalump as something which I
had created and nurtured much like my own child. Acting
somewhat like a careful mother, I planned a transition;
hoping that Heffalump would continue and thrive beyond my
involvement.

A large part of the transition was sharing the leadership and responsibility, which in the past, I had carried
alone. I chose to work together with Peter Wing and Bernie
Trilling. We formed a co-directorship and playfully refer-
red to ourselves as the "Triumverlump." Peter continued
from the previous year and Bernie joined Heffalump officially.

For a long time I had urged Bernie to work at Heffalump,
and finally, just back from traveling in Europe, he agreed. In
a sense he had always been involved over the many years. I
first met him when Heffalump began as Little Room, in a
space at his Stanford residence. Our friendship began then
too. In the handbook for the last year he described his
relationship:

> I have been happily Heffalumping from
> time to time, from musician to magician,
> Santa Claus to clean-up boss, just
> someone who cares, to just Bernie Bear.

Even without his furry beard, he was still known as "Bernie Bear" to everyone. With his six feet, four inch height, he brought to Heffalump a gentleness and warmth. Those qualities combined with a dancing bear humor delighted not only the children but parents as well. Bernie's musical talents created a new mood at Heffalump as story telling and meeting time were accompanied with all kinds of instruments. Throughout the year I gained much from Bernie. I learned to appreciate the need for a certain easygoingness in the midst of occasional chaos. Under his influence also, I found myself many times abandoning a half dozen items from my daily "things-to-do" list.

Working closer with Peter that year, I immediately discovered his tenacity and dedication. It was also a relief to share mountains of paper work with him. I appreciated his quiet, yet strong personality. His soft, listening approach to children was wonderful and I enjoyed watching him relate individually with a little one. Often he waited patiently until a child could express verbally an idea to him. Peter made humorous connections between words and actions which seemed to stretch images and relate the two in a special way. Many times his nonverbal inter-action with children through certain looks or signals produced instant giggles which rolled into uncontrollable laughter.

Together Bernie, Peter, and I began a collective venture. At first, sharing the directorship was difficult for me because I had been used to handling everything myself and had developed a personal style which felt comfortable. It was hard to let go and also admit to myself that I would be leaving Heffalump soon. In the beginning of that year I passed on my experience. Bernie and Peter were receptive to learning more about Heffalump and also seemed to understand my hesitation in making an immediate change in the directorship. After a short time of working together as a staff, my confidence and trust in Bernie and Peter grew and I found myself no longer having to carry the leadership role. The co-directorship as we had initially planned became a reality. I was relieved and happy to share the responsibility, knowing it was a necessary transition to insure Heffalump's continuation.

On the organizational side, Bernie took charge of bookkeeping and finances while Peter and I delved into paper work, program, newsletters, and parent involvement. We devised a rotation in which two of us would each work either in the morning or afternoon program for an extended period of time and the third person would float between sessions on a weekly basis. Extra parents scheduled themselves to participate in the session without the floating staff person. That plan enabled each of us to know all the children and parents well, and for the first time both morning and afternoon programs enjoyed a new continuity.

The three of us looked carefully at the inside space. By rearranging both rooms, we found that a few small changes made a large difference. Moving the loft to the carpeted end of the large room along with books, records, blocks, trucks, dress-up clothes, and musical instruments, opened that space for either quiet or lively group activities. In the opposite end of the other room we organized the remaining games, toys, art materials, science activities, doll house, and child-size kitchen. Since that area could be closed off by a sliding wooden partition, it became ideal for individual work and small group free play. I was pleased with the arrangement. Those simple changes seemed to enhance our program and also to suggest activities we had never tried. Best of all, the children liked the "new rooms."

While working inside we decided to reorganize the toy shelves. The impetus for that came from Peter's and Bernie's classes on the theories and methods of Jean Piaget and Marie Montessori. Bernie especially wanted to design independent learning devices for the children. Before developing anything new we decided to first sift through the many pieces and parts of toys we already had. We bought twenty-five clear plastic boxes with lids and organized the cluttered shelves. We were pleasantly surprised to discover that we had complete sets of many games, puzzles, and manipulative toys. The children reacted to the change as if everything were new. For the first few weeks the materials were in constant use and at the end of each day everything was neatly put away. Our beginning request to clean up was never repeated as the change seemed to imply a new order. We were pleased with the new skills some developed and the autonomy each child could enjoy.

Another addition to Heffalump was the establishment of a nap time. Since many of the children in the afternoon were much younger than previous years we created a special rest period. We purchased small aluminum and canvas cots and asked our families to contribute pillows and blankets. I introduced naps as something new but also in a matter-of-fact way. The children and I

discussed the rest time. Many of them talked about
giving up their naps at home and expressed that they did
not want to miss the fun at Heffalump for a silly rest.
Feelings were explored in the meeting but true emotions
were not revealed until that first nap period. Then
there was much resistance.

I realized immediately, that in addition to the
group preparation, nap time had to start individually. I
began very quietly and firmly with the most adament child
who also seemed to need to nap the most. I knew that if
I could get her to sleep, my chances of success with the
rest was almost assured. Between yawns and protests we
found her blanket and pillow and made up a cot in a
specially chosen place in the room. I acknowledged her
feelings and also reminded her that many of the other
children would soon be napping too. After asking if she
wanted a back rub, I began gently and requested that she
close her eyes. In a few minutes she was asleep. That
process was repeated and modified slightly with one
child after another until the whole room was filled with
sleeping little ones. After doing naps in that way for
about a week, I was able to get everyone on their cots at
the same time and stayed with the group until they had
all fallen asleep. Sometimes I read a quiet story or
played a soothing record. The best recordings I found
were from a nature series with sounds from the ocean, a
rain forest, and a meadow in the early morning. Another
good album was music arranged for Zen meditation.

The effect naps had on the whole program became
quickly apparent. Children looked more rested and
tension from being over-tired eased. The younger ones

played together better and parents began commenting on how much happier their children seemed in the evening after a long day at Heffalump. Soon, some of the older children began asking for occasional naps and helped set up the cots. For everyone, nap time became a pleasant and natural part of each day.

With the change to a co-directorship I found I could spend more time with the children on some personal interests. Building on the child-centered art and drama of previous years I began to encourage their own creative writing. Together we explored feelings, thought, and fantasy through the stories they created. Collecting those expressions, from both individuals and small groups, proved to be quite exciting.

One of our first projects became the children's newspaper. In a meeting to choose the name of the paper, a favorite and much used nonsense verse, "One and a two and a chick a bot a boo," was shortened to "Chick a Bot a Boo News." Each issue ran something from every child, be it a short story or a few words. On Thursday the issue was typed, illustrated, pasted-up, and duplicated for a Friday distribution. Some of the entries expressed three and four year old humor while others reflected serious insight.

Heather Hoppas   See that leaf spin-
                  ning. I think it's
                  going to get dizzy.

Kristel Bush   At nap time I had a
                  scary dream that a
                  King Kong monster put
                  my shoes on the wrong
                  foot.

Megan Hedgpeth	The fish died and food was his favorite thing.
Aaron Hertzmann	Everyday I really don't want my mom to leave, but actually it's ok.
Eric Baudelaire	Most babies get born at the hospital because there are tools in case the feet come out first.
Eden Mischkind	If I step on a balloon, it scares my ears.
Erick Richie	I hope my mom has a good wedding. She's going to have her honeymoon in our backyard.
Leia Stimpson	Heffalump is bubbling over with new kids.

Story dictation was a method I used to encourage children's writing. During the year that activity was expanded from written captions and descriptions on scribbles and paintings to lengthy tomes which developed from several days' worth of story telling. Each step of the process was exciting. Some of the children told their story very slowly and hesitantly, needing at times a few probing questions. Others rattled off a plot faster than I could write. All those creations were typed for Xeroxing or printed into books which many later illustrated. Stories were read and reread and became the special property of each child. Some

never tired of hearing their stories and brought them
day after day to be read outloud.
dictation a variety of writing was generated. Many
times familar fairy tales were modified with personal-
ized material. Dreams were collected and often fantasies
were woven from those dream fragments. Composite
stories were constructed with several children's ideas
and a cooperatively written play was produced that year.

While working with many of the older children on
their stories, I began seeing early signs of reading
readiness. Letters and words were recognized within a
familiar context. Though I had never thought of reading
when story dictation began, I quickly remembered a
teacher who taught reading exclusively from each child's
own words. In her book Teacher, Sylvia Aston-Warner
described her teaching experiences in New Zealand. The
available Dick and Jane type reading primers simply had
no relevance for her Maori children. Instead she exper-
imented by having her children create their own texts.
With each child she compiled a list of words. They were
printed, one to a card, and new ones were only added to
the stack if all preceding words had been recognized.
Since the words came directly from each child their
meaning had an obvious significance and were learned
readily. In time those word cards were shuffled into
sentences and reading commenced quite naturally. At
Heffalump reading sprang many times from a child's own
story. Though I did not consciously seek to teach
reading, our children like the Maori children discovered
reading through their own words. For those children
the magic that was released was exhilarating.

While at Heffalump I began to see the crucial need for child care. In spite of the many children's centers and preschools mushrooming around Palo Alto, waiting lists became common. In fact, parents with infants were often faced with a year's wait, thus requiring foresighted families the option of visiting centers long before their children were born. During the early years of the child care movement, Heffalump began as a small group which only met four hours a day. However, sensitive to our families' needs we expanded to a full day program while keeping our group uniquely small.

During that time I was quite conscious of the high cost of running an all day program and also aware of the large child care expense for many families. I pondered the issue of outside funding. While investigating funding sources I had a strong intuition that Heffalump should remain autonomous and self-supporting. It was a difficult decision to make as I saw many centers receiving corporate, county, and city money to start up new programs, to expand equipment and play areas, or to add to scholarship funds. I was uneasy with the idea of accepting outside money as I had seen some programs suddenly faced with a withdrawal of funding after many comfortable years and confronted at that point with no resources within themselves to make up the loss and continue as they had been. I wanted to maintain Heffalump's financial integrity and independence but I also wanted to continue a quality program and to help many low and middle-income families who were a part of Heffalump.

Fortunately, we found two programs which provided tuition subsidies for qualifying families. They were the

the Child Care Pilot Study and Palo Alto Community Child Care, (PACCC). I felt comfortable with the arrangement that the funding would go directly to families with Heffalump benefiting indirectly. For me, the distinction was important.

The Child Care Pilot Study was a research project passed by State legislation to study the need for child care and the existing services available in Santa Clara County. Many of our families of all income levels participated in that study. They simply reported monthly child care hours and fees and answered occasional questionnaires. In return they were reimbursed from 15% to 100% of their Heffalump tuition. The study continued for over three years and many parents received thousands of dollars of support. Later some of our other families who lived in San Mateo County became involved in a similar pilot study.

PACCC was another program which provided tuition subsidies. Begun largely from grass roots organizing in the early seventies, PACCC now operates with an annual budget of over $600,000. It obtains funding from a variety of sources with a little less than half coming from the City of Palo Alto. PACCC runs five large centers of its own and provides tuition vouchers for families in another seven centers and 20 day care homes. We applied for those subsidies and Heffalump was accepted as one of the seven voucher centers. Through the voucher program many of our families enjoyed full tuition support.

During the year we organized several fund raisers. The most successful was the New World's Crafts Festival in which we participated for the second year. With

Rivendell School, Camp Unalayee, and Creative Montessori
we set up a weekend fair in a grove of oak trees in a
city park. Led by Whitney Van Nouhuys and Jack Blackburn
we created a minature community with children's activities,
craft booths, food stands, music and entertainment.
Through Jack's special energy our festival attracted
exquisite and unusual crafts not often seen at local fairs
and a variety of music ranging from a Renaissance and
Baroque recorder group, a jazz trio, an Indian sitar
player, a belly dancing troupe, an Irish harpist, folk
singers, to five conga drummers, to name a few. There
were also wandering jugglers and mimes, palm readers,
and Sufi story tellers. People gathered around a small
hill to listen to poetry or simply watch others at the
fair. Dogs and babies slept in the shade while small
children with painted faces ran around with balloons
tied to their arms and food in their hands.

Heffalump parents worked long hours that weekend.
With members of the other groups they sold tickets, fixed
amplifiers, set up banners and parachutes, blended smoothies,
flipped quesadilles, and handled countless, unforeseen
details. Working together, a sense of satisfaction grew
as the fair continued.

Sharing all aspects of the fair, from the many months
of preparation to the final cleanup, heightened a feeling of
togetherness. Several days after the New World's Crafts
Festival, some of us met for dinner. The fair was carefully evaluated for the next one and the profits were
equally divided among the four groups.

The rest of the year raced on before I realized where
it had gone. Peter, Bernie, and I met to discuss Heffalump's

future. Peter was eager to stay on and work together
with his wife, Melinda. With that important matter
settled, I felt a little closer to leaving. We also
planned a six year reunion for everyone who had ever
been involved with Heffalump.

The reunion began, with an overnight at Foothills
Park. The next day others joined us for a picnic,
volleyball, and hikes. Stories and memories were shared
as some people had not seen each other for years.

After the weekend, I tried to cram all those
special things I had meant to do all year in that last
short week. The inevitable last day came and I gathered
support from both Ori and Bernie. Ori did not want to
miss the party and Bernie was sensitive to my feelings
and seemed to know when I needed an arm around my
shoulder. The children and I said good-bye with lots
of hugs and I felt myself saying good-bye to my
Heffalump years.

I hugged Peter a teary good luck and left hand in hand
hand with Ori. As we walked through the yard I was
quiet and absorbed in thought. Ori broke into the
silence and said, "Well, I guess we never did find
that Heffalump!"

I laughed and suddenly understood everything in
that unexpected moment. All I could tell her then was
that she was partly right but not entirely. I continued
mumbling out loud that Heffalumps were really never
meant to be caught. But all the years of looking had
actually become the heart of what could be found;
Heffalumps did, indeed, exist! Ori seemed to understand
as she squeezed my hand. I turned to her and caught a

mischievious look and heard a threat of last one there being a rotten egg. And then we raced each other to the car.

HEFFALUMPERS

Children

Patricia Adelmann

Karl Albrecht

Ori Anholt-Johnson

Ethan Artunian

Amanda Bermann

Amy Blething

Tatiana Bliss

Emily Breed

Jacob Bricca

Marion Briggs

Jenny Brown

Jesse Brown-Bentz

Rachael Brod

Kristel Bush

Annelise Chilton

Andy Costell

Steve Costell

Kiersten Crukshank

Oak Dellenbach

Seth De Fillippi

Matt Eddy

Donna Eyal

Matt Farrell

Alexis Ferris

Heather Flegal

Shawn Gantt

Joshua Greene

Kristina Grimm

Michael Grishaver

Davi Grunstein

Anastasia Hawkin

Moshe Hecht

Chris Hedgpeth

Megan Hedgpeth

Aaron Hertzmann

Dove Heider

Sara Hinkley

Steve Hinkley

Heather Honea

Heather Hoppas

Avram Hornic

Benjamin Hornic

Lara Hubermann

Darton Ito

Heather Jeavons

Kiersti Kaldveer

Usma Khan

Olav Knutsen

Jason King

Rafi Kuglar

Marisa La Dou

Kala Lawson

Adele Levy

Tania Love

Uriah Lovelycolors

Andre Marchand

Daisy Martens

Alicia Martinez

Christina Martinez

Erin Mast

Danny Melnick

Anna Meyer

Eden Mischkind

Cisco Moore

Irene Chique Moore

Atticus Munro

Adam Muse

Micha Mc Cann

Erin Mc Guigan

Amanda Mc Intyre

Nadja Mc Neil

Clay Mc Lachlan

Patchen Noelke

Carmelita Nocedal

Lija Nollendorfs

Ryan Ojackian

Rebbecca Parker

Erick Richie

Kim Richie

Christopher Rispoli

Phoebe Rossiter

James Sampson

Sean Savage

Jeff Scarvie

Will Scarvie

Gabriel Scurlock

Augie Seccombe

Jennifer Seidman

Josh Shulkin

David Sloan

Ariana Smart

Josh Smith

Josh Snodgrass

Peter Sonsini

Mandy Stafford

Leia Stimpson

Carter Strain

Tai Swenson

Muffy Taylor

Simon Troll

Boreas Van Nouhuys

Rusty Weaver

Andrea Westrum

Nina Wolgelenter

Sara Wood

Guy Yarvin

Ellie Yawata

Brynn Yeagar

Michael Young

Skye Zontine

Staff

Uni Victoria Anholt

Anne Branch

Dan Gurney

Bernie Trilling

Kay Vavuris

Ruth Vavuris

Peter Wing

Part-Time Staff

Agnetha Berg

Patti Bricca

Mary Ann Fisher

Shira Barnett

Jean Nixon

Jodi Ranuio